Fish-it 8

Norfolk

Published by:
Arc Publishing and Print
166 Knowle Lane
Sheffield S11 9SJ

Produced By: Chris Keeling

1

ISBN: 978-1-906722-25-8

ACKNOWLEDGEMENTS
I would like to thank the following for their
help in producing this guide:

Carl and Alex Smith for the great photo on the front page,
have a look at their website: carlandalexfishing.co.uk

All fishery owners who have kindly
provided information.

November 2012

Arc Publishing and Print
166 Knowle Lane
Sheffield
S11 9SJ

W E L C O M E

.....to the eighth book in the Fish-it series. Researching for this Norfolk book really opened my eyes to what a beautiful part of the country it is. Not to mention the quality of the the fishing venues that are scattered around the whole county. From Chapel Road Lakes in the north to Airfield Lakes in the south, there is something for every angler. It can be difficult to decide which one suits your way of fishing. Hopefully this guide will help you choose the right water for you.

Like many other anglers, my time on the bank is limited, but I like to grab a few hours fishing whenever and wherever I can. Always bearing this in mind, I have put together, my eighth book "Fish-it 8 Norfolk".
I have included all the details you need to find the venues and hopefully give you an idea of what's on offer at each, before setting off on a lengthy (and now with petrol prices so high) expensive journey.

Fishing attracts so many people; perhaps it is the solitude in often beautiful surroundings, or the eager anticipation of catching a big one! The bank side can be almost hypnotic and the desire to catch just one more fish has spoilt many a meal.

I hope you find this book useful and wish you good luck, good fishing and remember - "A bad day's fishing is still better than a good day's work!"

Chris Keeling

C O N T E N T S

ACKNOWLEDGEMENTS 2

WELCOME / CONTENTS 3

ABOUT THIS GUIDE......................................4

SPECIES / SYMBOLS.....................................5

KNOTS 6

POLE FISHING FOR THE BEGINNER..........7

FISHERY LOCATION MAP 8

FISHERIES 9

RIVERS 48

FISHING THE NORFOLK BROADS 50

FISHING TACKLE SHOPS 55

LOG-IT 56

FISHING TERMS 59

INDEX 62

NEW FISHERY / UPDATE FORM................63

A B O U T   T H I S   G U I D E

To help you locate a fishery, the venues have been arranged
in alphabetical order and split into two sections.
Their approximate location has been indicated on a map on
page 8

Blue Section   Norfolk fisheries

Red Section   Norfolk Broads and Rivers

Each page contains details of a fishery,
with information on the following:

Ticket Price: All day ticket costs plus details on OAPs,
                        disabled and junior concessions.

Directions: Usually from the nearest city or town, or
                        from the closest motorway junction.

Description: A brief outline of what the fishery looks
                        like plus details on features such as
                        islands, depths and the best
                        places to fish.

Types of Fish: List of species present, many with
                        estimated weights.

Rules/Bans: The restrictions set by the fishery
                        on type of baits, hooks etc.

Number of Lakes: The number of waters available to
                        fish at the venue.

Facilities: What is available at each location
                        i.e. cafe.

Telephone: The number of either the owner, angling
                        club secretary or match organiser.

Sat Nav: Post codes for use on satellite
                        navigation systems.

S P E C I E S / S Y M B O L S

Most commonly found in the Norfolk area.

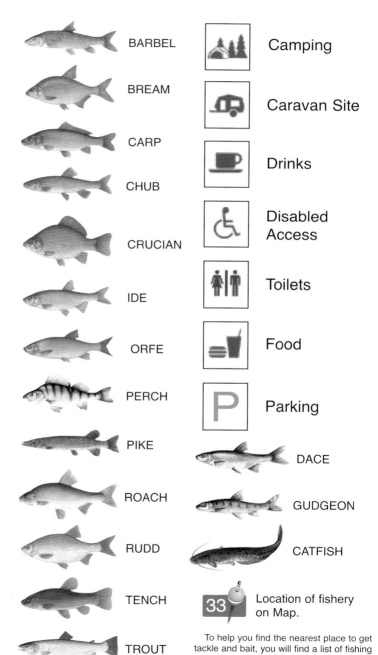

BARBEL

Camping

BREAM

Caravan Site

CARP

Drinks

CHUB

Disabled
Access

CRUCIAN

Toilets

IDE

Food

ORFE

PERCH

Parking

PIKE

DACE

ROACH

GUDGEON

RUDD

CATFISH

TENCH

33 Location of fishery
on Map.

TROUT

To help you find the nearest place to get
tackle and bait, you will find a list of fishing
tackle shops in the Norfolk area on page 55

Blood Knot

This knot can be used to join two lines together, start by overlapping the ends of the two lines.

Twist one end round the other line four times and pass it between the two lines.

Do the same with the other end of line, making sure the previous step does not come undone.

Before pulling tight wet the knot to lubricate this also make it hold better. Trim off the two ends.

Pull on the loose end to tighten. Trim the line.

Half Blood Knot

Used mainly for joining hook to line.

Thread the end of your line through the eye of your hook.

Pass the free end underneath the line and bring it back over the line to form a loop

Continue to loop the free end over the line about four times.

Pass the loose end between the eye of the hook and the first loop.

Double Overhand loop

This knot is used to create a loop at the end of a line. Also known as the surgeon's loop.

To begin, double the end of the line back against itself.

Tie an overhand knot in the doubled line.

The doubled end should then be tucked through the loop again.

Pull the knot as tight as possible and trim of the end.

Water Knot

This knot can also be known as the surgeon's knot. It is useful for joining a lighter hook line to your mainline

Hold the ends of the two lines alongside each other so that they overlap by about six inches.

Take hold of the two lines and make a wide loop.

Holding the two lines together. Pass the ends of the line through the loop four times.

Pull the lines tightly so that the loop makes a knot. Trim the two ends.

POLE FISHING
FOR THE BEGINNER

Of all the different methods of fishing I've tried, I haven't found any of them as accurate or as easy as pole fishing. To be able to place your bait and feed to the exact spot, sometimes only inches from an island or group of reeds is what makes pole fishing so productive and great fun.

TACKLE NEEDED

A Pole
Poles come in various sizes, from 4 metres (usually called a whip) to poles of 18.5 metres. They also vary dramatically in price as well, this is usually governed by weight and rigidity. The lighter and straighter (no droop at the end) the more expensive they are. I recommend a pole between 11 and 13 metres, stay away from the smaller telescopic ones. Many tackle shops have poles ready assembled for you to handle. Make sure you are comfortable with its weight and it feels well balanced. Test that it takes apart smoothly. If possible, get a pole with a spare top section as they enable you to rig up for different species and size of fish.

Pole Rigs
Experienced anglers can make up their own pole rigs but beginners are advised to buy ready-made. There are plenty of quality ready made rigs available for as little as £2.99. These rigs come with a main line with a loop on the end (used to attach the line to the stonfo connector at the tip of your pole). A float with enough shot below it to cock it nicely in the water and a length of lower breaking strain line, which has a spade end hook tied to it. The float and shot can slide down the line and be adjusted accordingly.

Pole Elastic
The elastic that runs through the top sections of your pole cushions the fight of a hooked fish and allows you to play it. Elastics are graded in sizes 1-20.
The following list is a good guide for the beginner:
1. For small roach and perch for example - use a No4 elastic with a 1lb hook length and a 2lb main line.
2. If fishing for small carp and tench or skimmer bream use a No8 or 10 elastic with a 3.5lb main line and 2.5lb hook length.
3. When fishing for carp up to 12lbs use a No16 to 18 elastic, and a main line of 8lb with a 6.5lb hook length.

START TO FISH

Fishing Position
Get your seatbox in position. Ideally, when sitting on the box, your thighs should be in a horizontal position, at right angles to your lower leg. Holding the pole correctly makes it comfortable for long periods and prevents backache. For a right handed person you need to rest the pole across your knees with your left hand supporting it. Put your right forearm along the end of the pole and firmly grip the pole with your right hand. Have close to hand - your bait, landing net, disgorger and anything else you may require for your days fishing. It is important to have your pole roller in the correct location. The pole has to be well balanced in your hands when it leaves the roller - this prevents rig tangles when shipping out.

Start Fishing
You have set up your pole and plumbed your depth - so now you are ready to fish. Make sure you have between 10" and 20" of line between the tip and float. In more windy conditions you may want to lengthen this. Feed your swim with groundbait (if allowed) plus a few bits of your hook bait. This is more accurately done using a pole cup which can be fixed to the end of your pole. Put your bait on the hook and ship out your pole trying to keep your rig in the water as this prevents tangles. Lay the rig on the water lengthways. The shot on the line will pull the line under the water and cock the float.
Enjoy your first pole fishing day!

Fishery Location Map

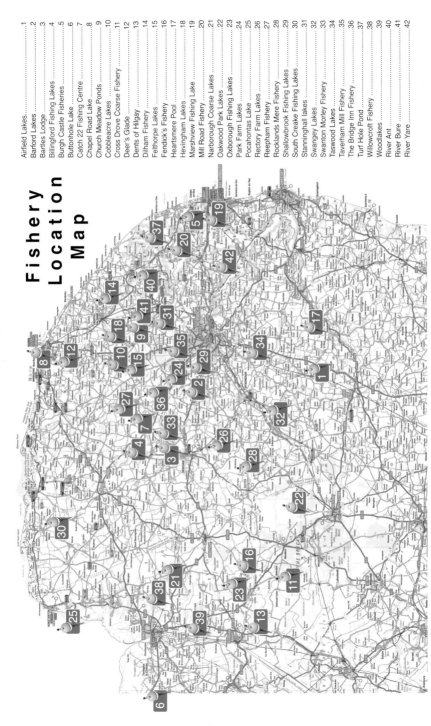

Airfield Lakes 1
Barford Lakes 2
Bartles Lodge 3
Billingford Fishing Lakes 4
Burgh Castle Fisheries 5
Buttonhole Lake 6
Catch 22 Fishing Centre 7
Chapel Road Lake 8
Church Meadow Ponds 9
Cobbleacre Lakes 10
Cross Drove Coarse Fishery 11
Deer's Glade 12
Dents of Hilgay 13
Dilham Fishery 14
Felthorpe Lakes 15
Fendick's Fishery 16
Heartsmere Pool 17
Hevingham Lakes 18
Marshview Fishing Lake 19
Mill Road Fishery 20
Narborough Coarse Lakes 21
Oakwood Park Lakes 22
Oxborough Fishing Lakes 23
Park Farm Lakes 24
Pocahontas Lake 25
Rectory Farm Lakes 26
Reepham Fishery 27
Rocklands Mere Fishery 28
Shallowbrook Fishing Lakes 29
South Creake Fishing Lakes 30
Stanninghall lakes 31
Swangey Lakes 32
Swanton Morley Fishery 33
Taswood Lakes 34
Taverham Mill Fishery 35
The Bridge Inn Fishery 36
Turf Hole Pond 37
Willowcroft Fishery 38
Woodlakes 39
River Ant 40
River Bure 41
River Yare 42

Airfield Lakes
New Lodge Farm, Dickleburgh, Diss.

Ticket Price: Mustang Lake: Day-Ticket Tariff.
£10 for 12 hours 2 rods. £12.50 for 12 hours 3 rods
£20 for 24 hours 2 rods. £25 for 24 hours 3 rods
Non fishing guests (only one per angler) £2.50 for 12 hours
and £5 for 24 hours. Spitfire Pool - Exclusive for week
bookings only.

Directions: At Kings Lynn take the A140 to Downham Market.
Pick up the A134 towards Thetford, then take the A1066 to
Diss. Next take the A143 towards Gt Yarmouth. Change onto
the A140 to Norwich. At the 3rd roundabout after Diss take
the 3rd Exit. Finally, before you go into the village take the
first turning right into common road opposite the Manor
House which is sign posted to the 100th Bomb Group
Museum. The fishery is just under a mile up this road on
your left.

Description: Mustang Lake has 14 well-drained comfortable
swims on the lake with excellent access. Two of the swims
are for short range fishing only, the rest allow you to cover
good chunks of the lake which suits easy medium range
tactics. Because these fish are young and fast growing
they do like bait and the anglers that do best tend to
bait up regularly to keep the action coming. Top quality
boilies, pellets and corn seem to be most effective.

Rules/Bans: On no account are the following to be brought
onto the fishery: Landing Nets, Unhooking Mats, and Slings.
The fishery will provide all of the above for you.
See fulll rule details on site.

Facilities: P **Number of Lakes:** Two

Telephone: Tel: 07706 48 30 84   Sat Nav: IP21 4PH   1

Barford Lakes

Chapel Street, Barford, Norwich.

Ticket Price: Adults: £8.00. Juniors/OAP/Registered Disabled: £6.00. Beginners Session (training lake only): £2.50.

Directions: From the A1, head for Norwich until the Thickthorn Services roundabout. Turn left onto the A47 - second exit on the roundabout, heading towards Swaffham. Continue to the next exit signposted B1108 to Watton and take this exit following the signs for Barford. After entering Barford you will see a pub called The Cock Inn. Take the road opposite which is Cock Street. Turn right at the T-junction and carry on through the village for about a quarter of a mile. On the right and you will see a gravel driveway, signed Barford Lakes.

Description: The Pleasure Lake is an attractive two and a half acre lake with mature bank planting offering good cover and privacy. It's well stocked with mirror, common and ghost carp into the high teens with the majority of fish weighing around the 6–10lb mark. There are 35 permanent pegs, 30 of which are spacious wooden pegs ideal for two anglers, such as father and son. Try caster fishing for the roach and rudd.

Number of Lakes: Eight lakes in total. Four on site. Four near by.

Rules/Bans: Barbless hooks only, max size 8. Two rods max (bite alarms allowed on silent only). No keepnets, dogs, loud radios or floating pole method. Un-hooking mats must be used. No Peanuts. Groundbait allowed - 2 kilo limit. Barford Lakes Carp Pellets only.

Facilities: ♿ 🅿 🍴 🚻 ☕ Tackle Shop 2

Telephone: 01603 759624   **Sat Nav:** NR9 4BJ

Bartles Lodge

Church Street, Elsing, Dereham.

Ticket Price: £8 per day. £6 concessions.
Residents - £6.00 per person per day.

Directions: From from Kings Lynn take the A47.
Continue towards Norwich past Dereham. Take the exit at
North Tuddenham where you will see a sign to Elsing.
Follow these signs to the village. You'll find the fishery
opposite the church.

Description: Bartles Lodge has three lakes - Victoria, Laura
and Lizzie – each approximately an acre in size. They are
spring fed with depths ranging from 2 to 8 feet. All are well
stocked with both mirror and common carp (up to 20lb)
tench, bream, perch, rudd and roach. Laura's lake (pictured)
can be fished with a float or ledger and the best baits to use
are bread, maggot, sweet corn and meat but most baits are
worth a try.

Types of Fish:

Rules/Bans: Barbless hooks only.
Unhooking mats to be used.
No keep nets (matches only) No bait boats. No night fishing.

Facilities: Some baits are available on site.

Sat Nav:
NR20 3EA

Number of Lakes: Three   **Telephone:** 01362 637177

Billingford Fishing Lakes
Elmham Road, Billingford.

Ticket Price: Day Ticket (7am-7pm) - £10.00. Overnight Ticket (24hrs) - £20.00.
Fly Fishing (One Lake + River)- £20.00 including 4 fish.

Directions: From Norwich, take the A1067, Fakenham Road through Lenwade past Bawesdwell Garden Centre (approx. 14 miles). Take 2nd left after Garden Centre, B1145 towards Billingford. Follow the road through Billingford and the entrance is just past the last house on the left.

Description: Billingford has 3 well stocked lakes of 7, 12 and 15 acres and 1 mile of the River Wensum. Despite being in existence for 20 years the lakes have rarely been fished, allowing wild carp stocks to flourish. Most have never been caught, providing a real challenge for the keen angler. The lakes each have shallow marginal shelves with depths of 8ft-12ft of water out from the bank to a 30 yard cast. Species include roach, perch, eels, pike, tench, bream. The 1st lake has a prolific head of common and mirror carp in the 10-25lb bracket. The middle lake is specially designated for fly fishing and is well stocked with both brown & rainbow trout and also some coarse fish that will take a fly.

Rules/Bans: See information on site. No dogs.

Number of Lakes: Three

Facilities:

Telephone: 01603 261012   **Sat Nav:** NR20 4RF

Burgh Castle Fisheries

Butt Lane, Burgh Castle, near Great Yarmouth.

Ticket Price: Main Lake - 2/3 rods costs £10 per day.
£15 per 24hr. Silver Birch - £5 per rod per day.
Kingfisher - 1 rod costs £5 per day. 2 rods costs £7.50.
1 rod costs £10 for 24 hours. 2 rods cost £15 for 24 hours.

Description:

Directions:

The Main Lake is for specimen carp fishing.
It has a tendency to throw up large commons in the 25-36lb bracket which are scale perfect.

This lake is around 1.5 acres, although not a large lake in carp fishing terms, there is still a few swims to get out of the way from the main crowd. The lake has lots and lots of features to fish, from reed beds, lily pads, two islands and a main gravel bar.

Silver Birch is the pleasure/match lake, which is around 3/4 acre in size. This lake holds a good head of smaller carp from 1-8lb. You never know what you are going to catch next in this lake, as there are teems of brown and orange goldfish, chublets, roach, rudd, perch, skimmers, specimen sized tench and the odd grass carp.

Kingfisher Lake is around 3/4 acre in size and contains carp from 2-18lb, a few good tench and plenty of silver fish.

Rules/Bans: Barbless hooks only. No keepnets. Landing nets must be used. Do not use rags when unhooking fish.

Number of Lakes: Three   **Telephone:** 0791 9080961

Facilities: Sat Nav: NR31 9PY

Buttonhole Lake
Rands Drove, Marshland st James.

SAT
PE14 8HA
NAV

Ticket Price: Day tickets £6.00. Under 16s £3.50 Under 12s must be accompanied by an adult.

Directions: Once at Marshland St James turn at the cross road onto School Road (next to Hickathrift Residential Home) carry on to the Marshland Arms pub. Directly opposite is Rands Drove which leads to the lake.

Description: Buttonhole Lake has been established for 12 years, with a relaxed atmosphere in the open countryside. It is a small well stocked fishing lake containing 24 wooden platform pegs and a central island. The average depth is between 4 and 5 feet. Margin fishing for carp with meat next to the reeds was working well for many anglers. During the summer try surface fishing with bread or dog biscuit in the evening for carp.

Types of Fish: Mirror carp to 20bs. Common carp to 15lbs. Ghost carp to 8lbs. Crucian carp to 2lbs. Grass carp to 15lbs, F1 carp to 2lbs. Tench to 13lbs. Barbel to 7lbs. Roach. Bream to 11lbs and perch.

Rules/Bans: No boilies. Barbless hooks only. No keepnets. Max hook size 12. No litter. Dawn till dusk. No bloodworm or joker.

Number of Lakes: One

Telephone: 01945 430629   **Sat Nav:** PE14 8HA

Facilities:

Catch 22 Fishing Centre
Bunnetts Lake, Lyng.

SAT NR9 5BQ NAV

Ticket Price: Coarse Fishing Day Ticket Lake £5.00.
24 hours: £10.00. Carp Fishing Day Ticket Lake 7.30am -
7.30pm: £15. Concessions £10.00 (See other prices on site)

Description: The day ticket lake is a mature gravel pit of
twenty acres that's over forty years old. It has thirty three
spacious swims, thirty one of these being bankside swims.
Ten of the bankside swims are doubles having room for two
people. Depths range from eight to twenty-four feet and it
boasts many features including islands, bars and plateaus.
The majority of the fish stock is made up of carp imported
from Holland, predominately commons. It's also home to
mirrors and leathers. The carp average 23lb, with a lot of
anglers catching between 25-35lb fish. There have been a
few fish caught over the 35lb mark during 2011. Original
stocks of roach, perch, tench, pike, bream are also present.

Rules: See list of rules on site.

Number of Lakes: Two

Facilities: There is also a large
tackle shop on site.

Telephone: 01603 872948   **Sat Nav:** NR9 5BQ   7

Chapel Road Lake

Chapel Road, Roughton near Cromer.

Ticket Price: Day fishing on the bank £6.00 Adults, £5.00 Concessions (OAP) and Junior. Overnight fishing (by arrangement only) £10.00 Adults, £8.00 Concessions (OAP) and Junior. 24 Hours: £12.00 Adults, £10.00 Concessions (OAP) and Junior.

Directions: From Cromer head south on the A140 towards Roughton. At the roundabout turn right into Chapel Road. Your will find the fishery on your left.

Description: This well run little fishery is ideal for all ages of angler. The two acre lake has feature islands to target as well as reed beds near most pegs. There are some large carp to 26lbs that are regularly caught using hair-rigged boilies or pellets. It also holds some good barbel to 6lbs, tench and bream to 5lbs. Crucian, perch, rudd and roach all reach the 2lb mark. A few huge eels have also been known to come out of this water. Most baits work here but on a warm evening try surface fishing with bread or dog biscuit.

Rules/Bans: No keep nets. Must use barbless hooks.

Number of Lakes: One

Telephone: 01263 761369

Facilities:    **Sat Nav:** NR11 8AF

Church Meadow Ponds

Hautbois Road, Hautbois.

SAT NAV NR12 7JW

Ticket Price: £5.00 on the bank
Night fishing by prior arrangement.

Directions: From Norwich take the B1150 to Horstead. Pass over the rail bridge and keep left towards North Walsham. Turn left into Hautbois Road, pass the church and the entry to the fishery is well signed, on your left.

Description: This privately owned, intriguingly irregular shaped lake spans around 4 acres and averages out at 4ft deep. It's a mixed fishery with carp to 41lb, some in the 30lb range and a good head of 20s - in fact the average size would hover around the 20lb mark. The venue also contains quality tench, pike and other species.
The bigger carp show to float fished tactics, although legering has its obvious claims. In the summer months try a bait like pellet, boilies, paste or slow sinking bread to the margins or the island sills. Given the right time of year and a warm day, float fishing can be extremely successful.

Types of Fish:

9

Rules/Bans: Barbless hooks only. No Keepnets.

Number of Lakes: One

Telephone: 01603 782453

Facilities:

Sat Nav: NR12 7JW

17

Cobbleacre Lakes

Brick Kiln Road, Hevingham

SAT NAV NR10 5NL

Ticket Price: Specimen Lake - Day Ticket: £10.00.
24hr Ticket: £20.00. Non-Specimen - Day Ticket: £7.00
Concession: £5.00. 24hr Ticket: £15.00

Directions: From Norwich take the A140 past the airport.
Take a left turn signposted Hevingham. Take your second
left into Brick Kiln Road and keep going until your see the
sign for the lakes.

Description: Adams lake is perfect for the carp angler who
likes to get a run, the lake contains no less than 200
doubles figure carp along with another 300 up and coming
young fish. The lake also contains carp to well over twenty
pounds so the fish of a lifetime is always on the cards.
Other stocks include large bream to 13lb, tench to 10lb+
along with a variety of silver fish.

Alex's Lake is what they call the fun pool, its around ¾ acre
and offers fabulous fishing. The specimen lake is called
Mario's and it contains thirty pound commons, mirrors,
leathers and ghosties plus catfish that reach 35lbs.

Rules/Bans: Every person must pay prior to commencing fishing.
Unhooking mats to be used at all times. The use of keep nets are allowed,
unless over wise stated. Carp may be sacked up for a short time whilst
preparing for weighing and photos. No fires allowed, gas stoves are
permitted. Please keep the lakes tidy. Any litter to be taken away with you or
placed in the bins provided next to the shop on the way out. No live or dead
baits to be used. No nuts or peanuts. Minimum 42 inch landing nets and
minimum of 12lb line to be used on Mario's lakes. 3 Rod max on Mario's, 2
rod limit on all other lakes. Barbless hooks on Adam's, Alex's, Amy's and
Gianna's.

Facilities:

Sat Nav: NR10 5NL
Telephone: 01603 754305
Number of Lakes: Six

10

Cross Drove Coarse Fishery
Cowle's Drove, Hockwold cum Wilton, Thetford.

SAT NAV IP26 4JQ

Ticket Price: £7 a day. Concessions £6.00. Evening £4.00

Directions: Take the A11 from Norwich. At Elvedon turn right on the B1106. When you reach Brandon turn left onto Main Street. At Hockwold cum Wilton take the B1112 for a mile the turn right onto Cowle's Drove. Continue until you see the fishery on your right.

Description: A beautiful looking lake with solid metal platforms. The lake has loads of islands and is not at all peggy, the quality of fish are superb with carp, tench, bream, f1's, catfish plus silvers. You can fish a match and not see another angler as the pegs are excellently placed with plenty of features. It is shut for 3 months over the winter to protect the fisheries banks and walkways but this can be checked by phoning first. There are toilets on site and a burger van serving hot food and drinks. You wont be disappointed by this fishery.

Rules/Bans: No keepnets except in matches.
Barbless hooks only. Please fish from the platforms only.

Number of Lakes: One

Facilities:

11

Telephone: 01842 828102   **Sat Nav:** IP26 4JQ

19

Deer's Glade

Caravan & Camping Park, White Post Road, Hanworth.

Ticket Price: One rod £4.50. Two rods £5.00
Children under 16 £2.50

Directions: From Norwich take the A140 towards Cromer. Five miles beyond Aylsham, turn right towards Suffield Green, signposted White Post Road. The site is 1/2 mile on the right.

Description: This is primarily a caravan and camp site with a reasonably sized fishing lake. The lake is well stocked with roach, perch, skimmer bream, carp and possibly other species but on the wet and windy day when we fished that was all we caught. If you can fish up to one of the two islands, then that's the place to be for the carp. Sweetcorn worked well with plenty of fish unfortunately none were over 5lbs but maybe I was just unlucky. My fishing mate stuck to using a maggot feeder and caught roach and perch all day. This is a great venue for families with kids as there is plenty of other things to do near by.

Rules/Bans: No keepnets. No barbed hooks.
See other rules on site.

Number of Lakes: One

Facilities:

Telephone: 01263 768633   **Sat Nav:** NR11 7HN

Dents of Hilgay

West Fen, Steels Drove, Hilgay, Downham Market.

SAT NAV PE38 0QH

Ticket Price: Day tickets are £6.00, with concessions available for anybody with a concessionary fishing license.

Directions: Situated just off the A10. Five miles south of Downham Market.

Description: The fishery comprises of 5 well-stocked fishing lakes. Farm Shop Lake is eight acres with 30 pegs. It is surrounded by reeds with a reed bed island. Prolific for crucians to 3lb and tench to 8lb, there are numbers of roach and rudd to 2lb-plus and a handful of carp to just over 30lb, which are not easily caught. Kingfisher Pond is quarter of an acre with 11 pegs and a mix of species with good nets of crucians, tench, chub, barbel and perch plus carp over 20lb. Best methods are pellet or corn under your feet. The three West Fen Lakes are found further down the Fen Road. Willows has one island and has 38 pegs with carp nudging 30lb, and a good stock of double-figure fish falling to boilies. There's a good head of silver fish with 60lb nets of roach and rudd making it great winter fishing lake on the waggler and feeder.

Types of Fish: **Sat Nav:** PE38 0QH

Rules/Bans: No keepnets, barbless hooks only. Other rules on site.

Number of Lakes: Five   **Telephone:** 01366 385661

Facilities:

Dilham Fishery
Chapel Rd, Dilham, North Walsham.

Ticket Price: Day Ticket £5.00. £1.00 Extra Rod. £4.00 O.A.P. £4.00 Under 16's (1 Rod). Under 16's must be accompanied by adult.

Directions: From North Walsham head south on the A149. Turn right as you enter Dilham onto Chapel Road. The fishery is half a mile on your left.

Description: Set in 2.5 acres, this 1 acre lake has 19 swims and is well stocked with rudd, carp and roach. It has been laid out to form an excellent commercial fishery and is well stocked with an abundance of coarse fish and is regarded as one of the best fisheries in the area. It's fed by a regular spring water supply meaning that the level of the lake is constant throughout the year. There are plenty of features to target including two central islands and numerous reed beds.

Types of Fish: Rudd to 1lb, tench to 5lb, mirror carp 1lb to 10lb, ghost carp average 3 to 4 lb some up to 10lb, common carp 1lb to 10lb, pure crucian carp to 2lb.

Bans/Rules: No keepnets, no artificial baits, groundbait or boilies, barbless hooks only, unhooking mats must be used.

Number of Lakes: One   **Telephone:** 01692 535592

Facilities: Sat Nav: NR28 9PZ   14

Felthorpe Lakes

Brick Kiln Road, Hevingham.

SAT NAV NR10 5NL

Ticket Price: Day tickets £7.00. Concession £5.00. 24hr tickets £18.00. Concessions £15.00

Description: Mirror Lake is also referred to as the specimen lake and is the largest at around 2 acres. It has many features and is stocked with several mirror and common carp in the twenties and late teens.

Directions:

Tench, roach, perch and rudd also feature. The record still stands at 26lb 10oz for a Common. Foxes Lake is an excellent day ticket water and it has got at least one 18lb common carp, a 9lb tench as well as smaller carp, bream, roach, rudd and perch. Shadows Lake, also called the match lake has 17 pegs and is well stocked. This is a good lake for small to medium size carp along with a good range of silver fish.

Types of Fish:

Rules/Bans: No keepnets. Barbless hooks only. More rules on site.

Number of Lakes: Three   **Sat Nav:** NR10 5NL   15

Telephone: 07765 258000   **Facilities:** ♿ P 🚻

Mirror Lake

Foxes Lake

Shadows Lake

Fendick's Fishery
Elmtree Farm, Northwold.

Ticket Price: £7.00 - Adult Day Ticket. £5.00 - Adult Evening Ticket (after 4pm) £5.00 - Childrens Ticket. £4.00 - OAP's Ticket. £15.00 - Night Fishing Ticket (up to 24hrs)

Directions:

Description: There are five lakes to chose from at Fendicks. Lake 1 is home to a good mixture of fish. In this well stocked lake you will find carp over 20lb, tench over 9lb and a variety of other fish including rudd, roach, and many more.
If Catfish are your thing, then lake 3 is definitely for you. It has over 50 in this lake, with the biggest catch of 2011 weighing in at 97lb! This lake is also well stocked with carp up to 36lb. It is also the biggest lake at Fendicks Fishery.

Rules/Bans: No keepnets, barbless hooks only.
Unhooking mats must be used.

Facilities:

16

Telephone: 07771 753163   **Number of Lakes:** Five   **Sat Nav:** IP26 5LE

Heartsmere Pool

Wortwell, Harleston.

Ticket Price: Pre-booking is advisable. £13 for 12 hours for up to three rods, plus £2 for a fourth rod.

Directions: Take M25 to the M11 North bound. Then take the A11 towards Norwich. Pick up the A14 to Bury St Edmunds and Ipswich. At Bury turn off onto A143 towards Diss and Gt Yarmouth. 10 miles past Diss at the second 'Harleston' Roundabout turn right, sign posted Redenhall & Wortwell. After 1 mile go past The Bell pub and garage on the right. At the caravan sign on your left, turn right into driveway.

Description: Located on the respected Waveney Valley Lake complex, Heartsmere Pool is a superb carp water which is two acres in size and averages 7ft deep.

Stocks include a good head of 20lb to 29lb carp. There are also tench to 10lb 8oz and a good head of roach and rudd to 1lb, plus winter pike to over 10lb. This lake holds some big carp so make sure you have the correct tackle.

Heartsmere is very popular in the winter months as bait is continually being fed into the lake. Some of the best catches are made at this time of the year.

Rules/Bans: No keepnets.
Many more rules on site.   **Number of Lakes:** One

Facilities: 17

Telephone: 01986 788 676   **Sat Nav:** IP20 0EJ

Hevingham Lakes

The Heath, Hevingham, Norwich.

Ticket Price: Adults £6.00 - two rods per person per day. Juniors £5.00 - two rods per person per day.

Directions: From Norwich ring road, follow the signs for Norwich Airport A140. Leaving the airport on your right continue to roundabout. Take first exit signed Holt B1149 and continue for about 5 miles until you reach the Marsham Arms public house on your right. Take next turning right sign posted The Heath. Continue until you see the sign for Hevingham Lakes.

Description: There are two waters which have been well established for over thirty years. Both are stocked with common, mirror and leather carp which are a good mix of single and double figures. Tench and bream to the 9lb mark and impressive roach to 3lb and rudd to a magical 3½ lb. The lakes are very well sheltered and have many features with reeds, over hanging branches, gravels and islands.

Types of Fish: Tench, bream, carp, roach and rudd.

Rules/Bans: Keepnets only in matches. Barbless hooks only.

Facilities:

Sat Nav: NR10 5QL

Number of Lakes: Two   **Telephone:** 01603 754368   18

Marshview Fishing Lake
Church Road, Burgh Castle.

SAT
NR31 9QD
NAV

Ticket Price: Day tickets cost £5.00. £7 for 2 rods. Night fishing by appointment only £10 per night. £15 for a 24hr ticket. Season ticket available at request.

Directions: From Great Yarmouth take A143 to the White Horse roundabout and follow the signs to Burgh Castle. After two miles turn right at the crossroads signposted to the village. Church Farm is then situated at the end of the road.

Description: This water is a widened reed - fringed dyke covering around three-quarters of an acre with depths to 8 feet. Contains roach, rudd, tench, carp, bream and perch. A good float water for youngsters and the family. Its an excellent water for catching carp on the pole. Great to have parking behind every swim, no tackle to carry, lovely reed fringed lake with nice bays to fish.

Types of Fish: Contains roach, rudd, tench, carp, bream and perch.

Rules/Bans: Barbless Hooks only.
No keepnets.

Number of Lakes: One

Telephone: 07983 726516

Facilities:

Sat Nav: NR31 9QD

19

Mill Road Fishery
Mill Road, Stokesby.

Ticket Price: Adult Day Ticket £5.00. Junior Day Ticket (Under 16) £2.50. Evening Ticket £2.50.

Directions: From Norwich follow signs for Great Yarmouth (A47). At Acle follow the signs for Caister (A1064). After 2 miles, crossing the River Bure. Take the first right after the bridge signposted for Stokesby. The Homestead is the first property on the right after approximately a mile. Turn right onto the track before the house. The fishery car park is 150 yards on your left.

Description: The lake is just under an acre and includes two islands which help to separate the anglers and ensure everyone has their own water to fish. The lake has 17 hand built wooden stages that provide flat, stable pegs. There is reputed to be one 20lb carp in the lake although there are confirmed fish up to 19lb and many doubles
There are also large numbers of tench that are gaining weight by the month. To provide something for everyone there is also a head of rudd and roach that provide the youngsters with good sport.

Sat Nav:
NR29 3EY

Number of Lakes: One   (Holiday accommodation available)

Facilities: **Telephone:**
Mob: 07917 756015

Rules/Bans: Barbless hooks only. Safe rigs must be used (no fixed leads or fixed feeders). Keep nets are not permitted. Only one rod to be used at any one time, no rod to be left unattended in the water. No nuts are allowed. All anglers fishing for carp must have a proper unhooking mat and an adequate landing net. No dogs are allowed on the site.
No children under 14 to fish without an adult. Children to be supervised at all times.

Narborough Coarse Lakes

Main Road, Narborough, Kings Lynn.

SAT NAV PE32 1TE

Ticket Price: Millers Lake is the Specimen Carp Lake and is only available via pre-booking. Millers is restricted to over 16's on day tickets and over 18's on 24hr tickets.
Day Ticket £9.00 (£2.00 discount from Tuesday to Thursday for OAP's) Foresters is the new coarse lake available to fish without booking. Minimum age 12 (must be accompanied by an experienced angler). 1 Rod £6.00. 2 Rods £8.00.

Description: Millers Specimen Lake is approximately 2 acres and has an island as a feature. The lake provides anglers with great sport situated amidst idyllic scenery creating a relaxing atmosphere but is predominantly for the carp angler with no pole fishing allowed. Foresters Lake is

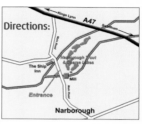

Directions:

newly opened. It is well stocked with smaller fish such as perch, roach, rudd, and chub whilst also containing a selection of medium to large sized carp. It has recently been stocked with several hundred crucians.

Rules/Bans: There is a list of rules for both Millers and Foresters Lake on site.

21

Number of Lakes: Two coarse, three trout. **Sat Nav:** PE32 1TE

Facilities: ♿ P 🚐 🚻 **Telephone:** 01760 338005

Oakwood Park Lakes

Black Dyke Road, Hockwold, Thetford.

 SAT NAV IP26 4JW

Ticket Price: Carp Lake (Per Person) Day Ticket £10.00 Night Fishing £15.00. Predator Lake day tickets need to be booked prior to fishing.

Directions: Oakwood Park Lakes is situated in the heart of the countryside some 6 miles north of Lakenheath and 25 miles northeast of Cambridge. The nearest two villages are Hockwold cum Wilton and Feltwell. If travelling from Feltwell locate the public house called The West End. From there head along Long Lane for 0.2 miles. Take the left hand turn into Black Dyke Road, continue along this road for 1.7 miles. You will then observe a sign for Blackdyke Barns on the right, continue around the bend, and there you will see an opening on the right hand side. Follow the signs and travel through the woods to where you will eventually reach the lakes.

Description: There are three lakes situated within the park. The predator lake is 4.75 acres with depths of 8-10 feet. It has large stock levels of fish ranging from catfish 120lbs plus and carp 35lbs plus. The second lake is about an acre which offers coarse fishing and is situated amongst the oak trees. The third and final lake is an ornamental lake that offers a picnic area for your enjoyment.

Rules/Bans: Far too many to mention. Make sure you view them at the fishery before fishing.

   22

Telephone: 01842 827812 - Mobile 07919 865 636

Facilities: P [🥤] [🚻]

Number of Lakes: Three

Sat Nav: IP26 4JW

Oxborough Fishing Lakes
Swaffham Road, Oxborough.

SAT
PE33 9PS
NAV

Ticket Price: Specimen lake - £10 for adults, £5 for second / third rods each. Small lake - £7 adults, £3 for second rod. Concessions £5 one rod £3 second rod. Concessions are for 65 and over and under 16 yrs.

Directions: From the A134 at Stoke Ferry take the turn to Oxborough, follow the road to Oxborough and the entrance to the Lakes is on the Swaffham Road in Oxborough.

Description: Set in picturesque countryside the Specimen Lake is 4 acres and has plenty of space between the 15 pegs. It is stocked with the famous Mockbeggar carp. All the fish in the Specimen Lake are 10lb plus with some fish around 20lb. The smaller 1 acre lake has 16 pegs and contains fish of a smaller size, up to 8lb, and is ideal for pleasure or match fishing.

Types of Fish: Bream, tench, carp, rudd and roach.

Rules/Bans: Barbed hooks are not permitted, No fixed leads or bolt rigs, No keepnets or sacks, all fish to be returned immediately. Un-hooking mats to be used.

Number of Lakes: Two

Facilities: Sat Nav:
PE33 9PS

Telephone: 01473 327366

Park Farm Lakes
Park Farm, Heath Road, Hockering.

Ticket Price: £7.00 per day ticket. £5.00 for concessions (OAP and registered disabled). Children under the age of 14 years must be accompanied by an adult. Holiday and late afternoon rates are available depending on the time of year.

Directions: From Norwich take the A47 towards East Dereham. After ten miles turn right to Hockering village. Turn right into Heath Road. After about a mile look for the fishery sign on your right. Take the lane down to the fishery.

Description: There are three lakes, Deer Park with 30 pegs at 6ft deep, Woodhouse with 20 pegs at 5ft deep and Copse with 15pegs at 4ft deep. All lakes have islands and are spring or stream fed. Simple tactics work best, float fish caster, maggot, pellet or corn for most species. Punched bread will get you plenty of roach during the winter months. Try fishing between the islands on Deer Park Lake for the carp. The key to success here is to feed little and often.

Types of Fish: Carp to 19lb, bream to 6.5lb, roach to 1.5lb, tench to 5lb.

Rules/Bans: Barbless hooks only. No keepnets.

Number of Lakes: Three   **Telephone:** 01603 881119   24

Facilities: [P] [♿] [🚻]   **Sat Nav:** NR20 3JA

Pocahontas Lake
Hunstanton Road, Heacham.

Ticket Price: Day tickets £7.50 for one rod. £2.50 for an extra rod. 24 hours £17.50 for two rods. Pre-booking is advised.

Directions: From King's Lynn head towards Hunstanton on the A149. When you reach Heacham turn left at the Lavender Centre. Turn first right and look for the fishery on your left.

Description: This 4 acre old estate lake is around 6 feet deep and has a small island in the middle.The River Hitch flows in and out of the lake keeping the water fresh. The lake has mainly specimen mirror, common, ghost and leather carp to 30lbs. Try feeder fishing for the large bream which are present with the average weight being 10lbs. Hair-rigged meat, pellet or boilies for the carp. The roach and rudd will easily be caught using punched bread, maggot or caster.

Rules/Bans: Barbless hooks only. No keepnets. Unhooking mats are compulsory.

Number of Lakes: One

Facilities:

Sat Nav: PE31 7HH to nearest house.

25

Telephone: 07876 151247

Rectory Farm Lakes

Watton Road, Hingham, Norwich.

Ticket Price: Day ticket £5.00.   Concessions £4.00.

Directions: From Norwich take the B1108 (Watton Road). Stay on this road as you go through Hingham. After about a mile turn left when you reach Wood Rising Road. You will find the lakes and camp site down the road.

Description: There are two lakes at the site, sporting mainly carp and tench. A smaller collection of roach, rudd, crucian carp and bream can also be found here. Both lakes are a simular size and depth, around 4 feet. They are well stocked with mirror, common and ghost carp, the largest being the mirrors at 20lb. Basic baits such as meat and sweetcorn work well for the carp. Worm will account for the bream and tench. If its quantity rather than size you want then fish maggot or soft pellet over a bed of micro pellets.

Rules/Bans: Dawn till dusk only. No groundbait. No floating baits. No boilies. Barbless hooks only.

Facilities:

26

Number of Lakes: Two   **Sat Nav:** NR9 4NN

Telephone: 01953 850596 Mob: 07919 530982

Reepham Fishery

Norwich Road, Booton, Reepham.

Ticket Price: Day-ticket fishing from the 1st March through to the 31st October (closed Mondays except Bank Holidays) Adults £9.00 - Concessions £7.00

Directions: Reepham Fishery is situated 500 yards south east of the market town of Reepham on the Norwich Road to Booton. If approaching on the A1067 that runs between Fakenham and Norwich, Reepham can be found by turning off at the B1145 Bawdeswell exit. The fishery is about 4 miles further on.

Description: Reepham Fishery has four lakes in total that are all spring fed and heavily stocked - the fishery is renowned for the quality and size of the crucian carp (up to 4lbs), together with tench to over 6lbs, roach to over 2lbs, rudd to 3lbs and carp to 28½lbs. Main and Long Lakes are joined to provide 3 acres of water with a total of 65 pegs stocked with mirror, common, leather, grass, koi, crucian and ghost carp, roach, rudd, tench, golden orfe.

Bans/Rules: Barbless hooks only. No keepnets.
Many people catch large poundages of a variety of fish some as large as 20+ lbs in weight. It is therefore essential that all anglers who wish to fish here come with a full set of equipment, and when they catch, they exercise great care landing and handling the fish, big or small.

Number of Lakes: Four

(Accommodation available on site.)

Facilities:

Telephone: 01603 870829   **Sat Nav:** NR10 4NR

27

Rocklands Mere Fishery
Chapel Street, Rockland St Peter, Attleborough.

SAT NR17 1UJ NAV

Ticket Price: Day ticket £8.00. Season ticket £100.00.

Directions: From Norwich, take the A11 heading towards Thetford. Bypass the turning for Attleborough town centre and take the next exit - signposted B1077 to Watton. Stay on this road for approximately 3 miles until you get into the village of Rocklands. There is a builders merchants in the middle of the village (Ridgeons). Take the next turning right past Ridgeons, this is Chapel Street. The track leading to the fishery can be found 800 yds on the right hand side.

Description: The Old Mere Lake is just over an acre in size and full of features. It lends itself perfectly to traditional float fishing tactics. Depths vary from 4 - 7 feet. Rocklands Mere Fishery is one of only a handful of waters in the country to hold true crucian carp. Most crucians are caught on waggler tactics with sweetcorn, bread flake, maggots and casters.

Rules/Bans: Barbless hooks only - Maximum size 8. No keepnets / carp sacks. Fishing is from dawn till dusk. Night fishing for season ticket holders only. Unhooking mats compulsory. No bait boats. No braided mainline. Fish from designated platforms only.

Number of Lakes: One coarse and one trout.

Sat Nav: NR17 1UJ

Facilities: There is a fishery lodge on site for angler's convenience and a well stocked tackle shop.

Telephone: 01953 483971
Mobile 07900 004953

Shallowbrook Fishing Lakes
Bridge Farm, Costessey, Norwich.

SAT NAV NR5 0LA

Ticket Price: Half day tickets are £4.00, 12 hours £6.00 and 24 hours £12.00.

Directions: Take the A1074 (Dereham Road) out of Norwich. At New Costessey turn right onto Norwich Road. Keep going until you see the lakes. The road goes between two of the lakes.

Description: The fishery comprises of 4 lakes which cater for all levels of fishermen from the novice to the experienced angler. Snipe Lake with its deep, dark water, lilly pads and reeds is a haven for tench up to 10lb and large bream. Roach and rudd are also in plentiful supply. Horseshoe Lake is reserved for match fishing only. Meadow Lake with its shallows and depths makes it an ideal water for all species. You can often find carp in double figures, tench to 7lbs and bream up to 10lbs all of which are in perfect condition. With a good head of roach, rudd and chub there is sport for all ages on Meadow Lake. This lake also has the added benefit of parking behind your swim. Carp Lake is secluded and surrounded by trees. This lake is where you will find the larger carp and is a favourite for the more experienced angler.

Rules/Bans: See details on site.

Number of Lakes: Four

Telephone: 01603 747667 or 07969 705777

29

Facilities: ♿ 🅿 🚻 🍴   Sat Nav: NR5 0LA

37

South Creake Fishing Lake
Compton Hall, South Creake, Fakenham.

SAT NAV NR21 9JD

Ticket Price: Day ticket costs £7.00 Adult, £5.00 Child (under 16 must be accompanied by an adult) and £5.00 for concessions. The day tickets can be brought on the bank.

Directions: The lake is part of Burn Valley Fisheries and is located just outside Fakenham on the B1355 heading to Burnham Market. Look out for the Compton Hall sign on your right and just after you have passed this take a left into Southgate Road. The fishery entrance is well sign posted on your right.

Description: The lake offers a wide range of fishing from the beginner to the most competent carp angler. The 3 acre lake gives you a chance to catch mirror and common carp as well as tench, roach, rudd and bream. The biggest carp caught weighed in at 28.9lbs. Many of the bream and tench are now reaching double figures. With a total of 25 swims this lake makes for a very good day ticket water.

Rules/Bans: Strictly no night fishing, keepnets, bait boats, fires or litter. Barbless hooks only. Nets must be dipped in dips provided. Landing nets and unhooking mats must be used at all times. Minimum line strength of 6lb. Maximum of two rods per person. Ground bait, pellets and particles are allowed but are restricted to 1kg every 5 hours per angler. No nuts.

Number of Lakes: One   **Sat Nav:** NR21 9JD

Telephone: 01328 823162 / 07771 660437

Facilities: 30

Stanninghall Lakes
Bay Willow Lane, Crostwick.

SAT NR12 7DB NAV

Ticket Price: Carp Lake (two rod limit) £10 (12 hours).
£20 (24 hours).
Pleasure / Match Lake £7.50 (2 Rods) £5 afternoon.
Predator Lake £7.50 (2 Rods) £5 afternoon.

Directions: From Norwich travel north on the B1150. Go
through Beeston. When you reach Crostwick village turn left
into Bay Willow Lane.

Description: The 2 acre Carp Lake holds some 220 carp of
which the split is 50/50 between mirror and common carp.
The lake features 9 swims and permits a maximum of 6
anglers at any one time. The current lake record sits at just
a fraction over 28lb. The Pleasure or match lake as it is
known is stocked with a wide variety of fish. The lake holds
tench to 9lb, carp to 16lb, crucian carp to 4lb, roach to
1½ lb, bream to 6lb, perch to 2lb and pike to 15lb.
Predator Lake is secluded at the far side and offers a real
treat for predator anglers with pike to 25lb
and perch to 3lb.

Rules/Bans: Two Rods only.
No carp sacks. Unhooking mats must be used. No keep
nets, No transferring of fish between lakes. No BBQ'S or
fires. No Bait boats. All Litter to be taken home.

Facilities: P ♿

Number of Lakes: Three
Sat Nav: NR12 7DB

31

Telephone: Mob: 07780 112174 Tel: 01603 784863

Swangey Lakes
Swangey Lane, Attleborough.

Ticket Price: Day tickets £7.00. 24 hours £15.00.

Directions: Come off the A11 at Attleborough. Take the B1077 away from Attleborough and after about one mile turn left into Long Street. After about another mile turn right onto Swangey Lane. Continue until you see the lakes on your left.

Description: A friendly family run business which boast 3 lakes packed with large carp, bream, tench and many small silver fish. The old gravel pits are ideal for leger or feeder fishing. Using meat worked well for the many double figure carp that are present. Big bream seem to be easily caught with sweetcorn. Maggot and caster for large bags of silver fish.

Types of Fish:

Rules/Bans: No Keepnets. Barbless hooks only.

Number of Lakes: Three

Facilities: Sat Nav: NR17 1XJ

Telephone: 07811 184154

Swanton Morley Fishery

Worthing Road, Swanton Morley.

Ticket Price: Day Ticket £5.00 - single rod.
Junior £3.00 - single rod. Additional rod £3.00.

Directions: From Norwich take the A1067. After 12 miles turn left onto the B1146, Dereham Road. After 2 miles turn right into Mill Street, then right onto Worthing Road.

Description: Dereham and District Angling Club run these 50 acres of gravel workings, split into two small and three large pits. Depth fluctuates between 3 and 20 feet and can vary within just a few feet, especially around the many bars and peninsulars. There is a superb stock of roach, including specimens to over 2lb, an increasing head of bream to 15lb and a fine head of tench between 3lb and 8lb as well as perch (including the odd whopper), crucian carp and common carp. Pike over 25lb are also caught most winters. Also on site is a super three quarter mile stretch of the River Wensum containing good roach, dace, chub and pike.

Rules/Bans: No night fishing. 7am - 7pm during summer months. 8am - 4pm during winter months Oct - Mar inclusive.

Number of Lakes: Five + a stretch of the River Wensum.

Facilities: **Telephone:** 01362 637591 33

Taswood Lakes

Mill Road, Flordon, Norwich.

Ticket Price: Carp lakes £10 for a day ticket, 7am to 6 pm. £20 for 24 hours.

Directions: Leave Norwich on the A140. When you reach Newton Flotman, turn right onto Flordon Road. Continue into Station Road. Turn left at the T junction. After half a mile you will see the entrance on your left.

Description: There are four main carp lakes, Spring, Grove, Heron & Broadwing, all of which are available to fish on a day ticket. The current carp record was set on the Broadwing Lake, where the ghost carp named the 'lady of the lake' was caught weighing in at a massive 41lb.
At Taswood three of the specialist carp lakes also have a strong head of hard fighting pike with the current record sitting at over 30lbs as well as some very large perch and eels. Like the carp lakes all the coarse lakes are well stocked and contain a variety of species to cater for all types of angler.

Types of Fish:

Number of Lakes: Eleven   **Telephone:** 01508 470919

Rules/Bans: Bailiffs conduct regular rig checks to ensure compliance to the rules as fish welfare is paramount at Taswood. See rules on site.

Sat Nav: NR15 1LX

Facilities:

Accommodation available in lodges. Tackle shop on site.

Taverham Mill Fishery
Taverham, Norwich.

SAT NAV
NR8 6TA

Ticket Price: Taverham Mill Lake - Day Ticket (2rods) £11.50

Directions: Taverham Mill Fishery is set on the outskirts of Taverham, approximately 5 miles outside of the historic city of Norwich. Head out of Norwich on the A1067. Turn left at the signpost for Taverham. Continue down Sandy Lane until you reach the fishery.

Description: The fishery is set in approximately 100 acres of fabulous Norfolk countryside and boasts 4 lakes and 3/4 mile of the famous River Wensum.

Taverham Mill Lake now boasts carp to over 30lb with loads of fish in the 20lb class. This lake also has some wonderful tench fishing and specimens to over 8lb are caught each season. It is approximately 23 acres, and is irregularly shaped with several islands and back channels. In the summer, the lake is covered by expansive patches of lilies, which always hold lots of carp, along with beds of Canadian pondweed, gravel bars and plateaux. Depths range from a few inches to 10 feet.

Types of Fish: Predominately Carp and tench with some silver fish and pike.

Rules/Bans: See list on site.   **Sat Nav:** NR8 6TA

Number of Lakes: Four (Only Taverham Mill Lake is day ticket)

Facilities: [P] [♿] [🚻] [🥤]   (Tackle shop on site)

Telephone: 01603 861014   35

Taverham Mill Lake

The Bridge Inn Fishery
The Bridge Inn, 2 Fakenham Road, Lenwade.

Ticket Price: Day tickets are priced at £7.50 and permits fishing with 2 rods on the "Bridge" lake as well as both the ponds and the river.

Directions: Head out of Norwich on the A1067 Fakenham Road. When you reach Lenwade look out for the pub on your right hand side.

Description: With 2 specimen lakes of 8 and 5 acres, 2 smaller carp lakes, 2 match/pleasure ponds and an enviable stretch of the fabulous River Wensum, the Bridge Inn Fishery has a water to suit most anglers. The Bridge Lake has common and mirror carp ranging between 12 and 37lbs. There's also tench to 9lbs, bream to 13lbs, pike to 26lbs, crucian, roach and perch. This mature gravel pit with an island, reed beds and depths of 4 - 10ft is a relatively easy carp water.

RULES OF THE FISHERY.

1. The Lakes, Ponds & River at The Bridge Inn & Hall Walks are Private Property.
2. All anglers must hold a current and valid Environment Agency Fishing Licence.
3. Day ticket holders are allowed to fish the Pub main lake, 2 match ponds and the River only.   Definitely NO FISHING on any of the lakes at Hall Walks.
4. Night Fishing is restricted to Season Ticket Holders ONLY . . . and is allowed on the 2 main lakes and the River. (There is NO night fishing on the 2 smaller lakes at Hall Walks or the match ponds.)
5. Day Ticket Holders – Fishing is from Dawn to Dusk only. (2 rod maximum.)
6. The maximum stay permitted in any one swim on the lakes is 72 hours (3 days.) The maximum stay permitted on the River is 12 hours and definitely NO bivvies.
7. A maximum of 3 rods to be used on the 2 main lakes, 2 rod maximum on the 2 smaller lakes and 1 rod only for the match ponds. (Never leave unattended.)
8. NO LITTER . . . Please take all your litter home, and ensure your swim is litter free.
9. No Bait Boats! No Wading! No Fires! No Dogs! No Nuts! No fixed leads!
10. No tree/swim cutting to take place or any damage to marginal plants or shrubs.
11. Definitely no livebaits to be transported to the Fishery. No Pike Gags or Gaffs.
12. Under no circumstances are any fish to be removed/killed, transferred from one lake to another or introduced to the Fishery.
13. Please respect our fish – No Carp, Tench, Bream or Pike to be retained in nets. Carp may be sacked overnight or for the minimum possible time for photographic purposes only and not for multiple capture photo's. (Please ensure that your sacked fish is in a good depth of shaded water.) Use only safe rigs. The use of suitable unhooking mats is compulsory.
14. Report all fish deaths or any sign of pollution to the Pub immediately. All fish, (even when dead), remain the property of the owners.
15. Strictly no publicity of any kind without the owner's permission. (This rule applies to any slanderous or libellous actions on fishing forums, talk forums or any other websites.)
16. Please respect the neighbourhood and refrain from using the access to the Fishery along "Hall Walk" between the hours of 10:00pm – 7:00am.

Sat Nav: NR9 5SE 36

Facilities:

Acommadation is available at the Inn. (Carp bait available)

Telephone: 01603 872248

Turf Hole Pond
Potter Heigham.

Ticket Price: £5.00 a day.

Directions: Take the A149 from Great Yarmouth towards Cromer. Once you have crossed the river at Potter Heigham take the first right into Station Road. At the junction pull into the farm yard and follow the sign to the fishery. The pond is 300 yards down the farm track.

Description: A traditional one acre mixed coarse fishery. It is packed with most species of silver fish with many carp some of which reach 23lbs. Bream reach 9lb, perch, roach and rudd all over a pound. Target the 8 - 9lb tench on the north bank on a sunny day with baits such as luncheon meat or sweetcorn for great results.
Great weights of roach and rudd can be had with single white maggot or caster.

Rules/Bans: Barbless hooks. No Keepnets.

Facilities:

Food outlet near by.

Telephone: 01692 670604   **Sat Nav:** NR29 5AD   **Lakes:** One

Willowcroft Fishery

Pentney Lakes, Common Road, Pentney, King's Lynn.

SAT NAV PE32 1LE

Ticket Price: Day tickets £6 per rod (all day fisherman have to leave the fishery by 7pm in the summer months and 1 hour before dark in the winter months).

Directions: From King's Lynn take the A47 heading towards Swaffham. Continue along this road and enter the village of East Winch. At the Carpenters Arms public house on the left hand side, turn right towards East Bilney. Continue along this road until you come to Pentney Lakes, which is signposted on the left hand side.

Description: Eight lakes to choose from that are all well stocked with carp, bream, roach, rudd, perch and catfish. Specimen Lake is 4.5 acres with depths down to 18 feet but an average of 12ft. It features plenty of gravel bars and is stocked with carp from 16lb to 34lb. Bream to 7lb, tench to 5lb, roach, rudd and pike to around 20lb are also present. The main baits on this water are boilies. Pellets on the Method feeder also work very well. For young anglers try the 'Under 16 Lake." It is half an acre in size and the shape of doughnut. Carp to 10lb, plus most other species are stocked. Pole fishing or waggler fishing with maggot produce the best results.

Rules/Bans: Barbless Hooks Only. For more information on current bans please check with bailiff.

Number of Lakes: Eight   **Sat Nav:** PE32 1LE
Telephone: 07551085415 or 01760444213

 38

Facilities:

Woodlakes
Holme Road, Stowbridge, King's Lynn.

Ticket Price: Weekend / Bank Holiday (No Concessions) £10
Monday to Friday £8.00
Concessions, Juniors and Residents £7.00
After 3pm (Monday to Friday) £5.00

Directions: From King's Lynn proceed south on the A10 passing through West Winch, Setch, Tottenhill and on to South Runcton. Turn right off the A10 into School Road at the sign to Runcton Holme and continue to the T-junction at the end. Turn left and continue for approximately half a mile and you will see Woodlakes on the left hand side.

Description: Woodlakes five tranquil lakes which cover 30 acres, were formerly gravel pits and have been used by anglers for over 50 years. All the lakes are well stocked with an array of fish including Carp (up to 40lbs in weight), roach, tench, bream, rudd, perch, pike and eels. For those after easier fishing there is the 4 acre Two Pole Lake with an abundance of common and mirror carp weighing into double figures.

Number of Lakes: Five

Rules/Bans: Barbless hooks only. All anglers must have a unhooking mat. No keepnets. Two rods per person. No nuts.

Facilities:  Accommodation is available on site in log cabins.

Sat Nav: PE34 3PX   **Telephone: (01553) 810414**   39

River Ant
Ludham Bridge.

Ticket Price: Free Fishing.

Directions: From Norwich take the A1151 to Wroxham. Go through the town and turn right onto the A1062. Continue on this road until you reach Ludham Bridge. There are parking spaces at either side of the bridge.

Description: Fish on the feeder to catch bream - chopped worm works well. Stick float with maggot, castor or hemp and tares to catch the roach. The depth varies on this stretch between 6 and 9 feet. You can also catch perch to 3lbs and the odd carp up to 16lbs have also be caught. Leger dead baits if you fancy a few winter pike which reach 30lbs. Top tip, fishing near the bridge is always good for roach.

Facilities: Toilet and refreshments nearby.

Sat Nav: NR29 5NY
To nearby pub.

River Bure
Coltishall Common.

Ticket Price: Free Fishing.

Directions: From Norwich take the B1150 to Coltishall. After you cross the bridge turn right. Follow the road for about a mile and look for the river and parking on your right.

Description: Plenty of roach can be caught fishing pole or waggler with maggot and caster. Feeder tactics with chopped worm again is still the favourite for the bream at around 6lbs. Good sized perch are coming out that reach 3lb. The river also holds some large carp and pike to 20lbs.

Facilities:
Toilet and refreshments nearby.

Sat Nav: NR12 7EA
To King's Head pub.

River Yare
Beauchamp Arms, Claxton.

Ticket Price: Adults £4.00. Children under 16 £2.00. Children must be accompanied by an adult.

Directions: If coming out of Norwich, take the A146 heading towards Beccles. At Thurlton turn left, signposted Claxton. Turn right and continue until you reach the Beauchamp Arms.

Description: This tidal stretch of the river has plenty of roach which reach nearly 3lbs. Dace to 9oz, a few hybrids and some large carp to 20lb. The main reason many anglers fish this stretch is for the large head of bream, with a some reaching double figures. The best tactic is to fish an open feeder with a strong scented ground bait with a red maggot on the hook. Pole fish down the edge for the roach again using maggots. Top tip, try fishing to the right of the pub for the bream.

Rules/Bans: Fishing is from dawn till dusk. No night fishing.

Facilities:  Toilet and refreshments at the Beauchamp Arms.

Sat Nav: NR14 6DH

Telephone: 07990 572729 or 01502 531776

Fishing on the Norfolk Broads

Where To Go Fishing on the Norfolk Broads

The region has lots of free fishing places and angling platforms along most of the river banks of the Broads and you can also fish from a boat. There are also Private Broads that offer fishing by prior arrangement and day ticket bank fishing spots. Always check with the fishery owner for detailed directions and permit information. However there are certain Broads where no fishing is permitted because they are conservation areas, and are signposted.

The Broads Authority also provide ease of access with fishing platforms for wheelchair users available at Rollesby Bridge, Filby Broads and on the south-east bank of the River Thurne (Martham) and upstream of the New Bridge at Potter Heigham.

Many of the Broads are not accessible by road and are private. Prior arrangement is necessary for those wishing to fish. Here are some of the Broads where you can fish, followed by the river coarse fishing that is available on the Norfolk Broads.

The Norfolk Broads are a fragile wetlands environment, so please take litter home with you and remember never to discard fishing tackle, as it can easily harm wildlife.

Alderfen - 15 acres of boat fishing only.
Barton Broads - 100 acres of fishing by boat.
Decoy Broads - Norwich AA.
Hickling Broads & Heigham Sound - 400 acres of fishing accessible by boat.
Horsey Mere - Must be accessed from Meadow Dyke. No boats for hire locally. Bank fishing limited to Horsey Village Staithe (tickets Staithe Store).
Little Bridge Broads - A small broad good at dawn and dusk.
Ormesby Broad - Rollesby, Lily, Great Ormsby and Filby.
Broads - 800 acres of angling waters not connected to the rest of the navigation. Best fished by boat.
Rockland Broad - Mostly boat fishing.
River Ant - At Ludham Bridge there is free fishing for 2.25 miles on the left hand bank both up and downstream of the Bridge.

River Bure - One of the major rivers of the Broads system, with certain stretches being very difficult to fish. Try Coltishall Common, Wroxham, Woodbastwick, Acle Bridge. Boats available in several places, boat hire available per day to non-members.

River Chet - Fishing is available from Loddon to Hardley Cross.

River Thurne - Short tidal river connecting several water courses. Good stretches of free Broadland fishing at Martham Ferry, Martham Boatyard and Potter Heigham.

River Wensum - One of Norfolk's loveliest rivers although mainly privately controlled. Free fishing at Fakenham Common. For other access around the riversides contact local tackle shops.

River Yare - Under-rated river, try Whitlingham, Surlingham Ferries, Buckenham, Cringleford Bridge. Permits for other areas from tackle shops in Norwich.

Wroxham Broads - 100 acres of good fishing. Has to be fished by boat from Wroxham Angling Club.

The Norfolk Broads, at 300 square kilometres, is one of Britain's best known angling locations and one of the region's premier tourist attractions.

The Broads is a good area for fishing where bream, eel, perch, pike, rudd and tench can be found. The coarse fishing season runs from 16 June to 14 March and all that you need to fish is a current Environment Agency Licence, available from post offices.

Fish found in the Broads area

Roach:
Average size 2 - 10oz
Broads specimen size: 1 1/2 lbs
Tackle: Float Fishing, waggler or stick. Ledger and swimfeeder in faster waters.
Baits: Bread, maggots, caster, sweet corn
Lines: 2lbs - 4lbs
Hook Size: 20 - 16

Rudd:
Average Size 4 - 10oz
Broads specimen size: 1 1/4 lbs
Tackle: Float Fishing, waggler set shallow.
Baits: Bread, maggots, caster, sweet corn
Lines: 2lbs - 4lbs
Hook Size: 20 - 16

Bream:
Average Size 2 - 3lbs
Broads specimen size: 7 lbs
Tackle: Float and ledger tackle fished on the bottom.
Swimfeeders are very productive.
Baits: Bread, maggots, caster, sweet corn, worms and groundbait.
Lines: 3lbs - 6lbs
Hook Size: 18 - 12

Pike:
Average Size 4 - 12lbs
Broads specimen size: 20lbs
Tackle: Powerful tackle required.
Baits: Fish baits float fished on and off the bottom and artificial lures.
Lines: 15lbs b.s. (min.)
Hook Size: Doubles or trebles. 8 - 6. Barbed or de-barbed.

Perch:
Average Size 4 - 12oz
Broads specimen size: 2lbs
Tackle: Float and ledger fished deep.
Baits: Worm, maggot, castor, small fish, small lures.
Lines: 2lbs - 4lbs
Hook Size: 18 - 12

Tench:
Average Size 2 - 3lbs
Broads specimen size: 5lbs
Tackle: Float and ledger fishing on the bottom
Baits: Bread, maggots, caster, sweet corn and worm
Lines: 4lbs - 6lbs
Hook Size: 18 - 10

Rules

Fish Care – retaining fish

If you use a keepnet:

Only use a keepnet when necessary and retain fish for the shortest time possible.

Make sure your keepnet is made of fish-friendly mesh and complies with local bylaws.

Don't overcrowd your keepnet, especially during hot weather.

Make sure there is enough depth of water for your net.

Place fish in the keepnet quickly and gently.

Large fish should not be retained in a keepnet.

Do not tow fish in keepnets behind boats.

Keepnets should not be left unattended for extended periods of time.

Ensure that your keepnet is secured properly to the bank or boat to protect it from the wash of motor cruisers.

Don't keep pulling the net out of the water to show off your catch, this will harm the fish.

Return your catch carefully, do not slide or tumble fish down the keepnet into the water.

Unhooking fish

Use barbless or micro-barb hooks where possible. They are kinder to fish and hook removal is much easier.

Carry several disgorgers (you will always lose one!) and forceps for the removal of larger hooks.

Always wet your hands before handling any fish. Do not use towels, wet or dry, as these can remove the protective slime from fish.

Be mindful of unhooking surfaces making sure they are soft and wet. Always use an unhooking mat on soft, flat ground for pike and large fish.

Fish should be weighed in appropriate nets or weighing slings and NOT by the gills.

When taking a photograph, have your camera ready before you take the fish out of the water.

When holding fish, always make sure you keep them low to the ground.

Fish should always be returned to the water quickly and gently after weighing (if this is necessary) or at the end of the day, if retained in a keepnet.

Fishing methods and unattended rods

Baits and lures should never be left trailing behind moving motor cruisers and day boats. This practice is not only ineffective it is also dangerous.

Pike fishing requires specialist knowledge and tackle. It should not be attempted unless you are confident that you can unhook and safely return your catch. If in doubt seek expert advice.

It is an offence to leave a baited rod unattended. It can endanger water birds and fish (particularly pike) which might gorge the bait or snag the line. There is also a danger from passing boats.

Be aware of crime, don't leave rods or other valuables unattended on the bank or boat.

Wildlife and the environment

Don't drop litter – use bins and disposal points.

Choose your swim with care to reduce the risk of snagging bankside trees, vegetation and obstacles in the water.

Take care where people feed waterfowl; the birds may have learned to associate people with food and their expectations will increase the risk of entanglement.

Remove rigs caught up in vegetation, branches or underwater snags immediately, where it is practical and safe to do so.

Beware of birds swimming into your fishing line. Swans can reach your bait one metre below the surface and other birds will often dive for food. Wind in your tackle if you think birds are at risk. Hooks and line should never be discarded, especially baited hooks. Line should be cut into one-inch lengths and disposed of with care or better still, taken home.

Safety

When fishing from hire craft, moor safely and always wear a life jacket.

Wear appropriate footwear on deck and always be mindful of slippery surfaces.

Be aware of power cables, especially overhead in boatyards or set back from banks.

Take notice of any warning signs. Look out, look up and cast with care!

Observe speed limits. Be considerate to other water users. Always watch your speed.

Other water users

Angling is very important to many people but it is just one of many legitimate water activities. Please respect the rights of other users.

If fishing near a bend in the river or amongst tall reeds be aware of approaching boat traffic, they may not be able to see you.

When fishing close to boats, be considerate and use a pole cup to place groundbait, rather than a catapult.

Should you accidentally get your hook caught on a boats mooring ropes, please don't leave it there to injure someone's hand. Remove the hook but make sure that it is safe and practical to do so. Ask the permission of people on the boat if it is occupied.

When fishing at moorings, anglers should give way to vessels trying to moor up.

Keep paths clear for pedestrians and cyclists.

Information kindly supplied by norfolkbroads.com

NORFOLK
TACKLE SHOPS

Angler's Corner. 22-24, Windsor Rd, King's Lynn, PE30 5PL   01553 775852

Angling Direct. 279 Aylsham Road, Norwich, NR3 2RE   01603 400870

Anglers World. 59 Long John Hill, Norwich, NR1 2JJ   01603 619381

Avenue Angling. 16 Denbigh Road, Norwich, NR2 3AA   01603 764004

Barford Lakes & Tackle Shop. Chapel St, Norwich, NR9 4BJ   01603 759624

Brights. 8 Wyndham St, Sheringham, NR26 8BA   01263 825858

Broadland Angling. 24-26 High Street, Stalham, R12 9AN   01692 580959

Complete Angling Ltd. Cess Rd, Great Yarmouth, NR29 4RQ   020 8144 4963

Cordy's Tackle Den. 390B Bowthorpe Road, Norwich, NR5 8AG   01603 250043

Darrow Farm. Shelfanger Road, Diss, IP22 4XY   01379 771009

Fakenham Angling. 35b Bridge St, Fakenham,NR21 9AG   01328 862543

Get Reel Tackle. 157-159, Reepham Rd, Norwich, NR6 5PA   01603 788470

Gorleston Tackle Centre Ltd. 7 & 8 Pier Walk, Great Yarmouth,   01493 662448

Howlett's Fishing. 53-55 High St, Downham Market, PE38 9HF   01366 386067

Hunstanton Tackle. 8 Greevegate, Hunstanton, PE36 6BJ   01485 535141

J.M.P Tackle. Unit 26, Haverscroft Ind Est, Attleborough.   01953 455282

Lathams Fishing. 1 Cherry Lane, Norwich, NR3 1WA   0845 3664646

P.M Pegg Angling Supplies. 22a Victoria Rd, Diss, IP22 4HW   01379 640430

Pownall & Son. 74 Regent Road,Great Yarmouth, NR30 2AJ   01493 842873

PW Angling. 59 Long John Hill, Norwich, NR1 2JJ   01603 619381

Shipshape Tackle. 7a Austin Fields, King's Lynn, PE30 1PH   01553 764058

Tacklemania. 20-22, Guildhall St, Thetford, IP24 2DT   01842 338187

Taverham Tackle Den. Costessey Rd, Norwich, NR8 6TA   01603 861014

Tim's Tackle. 71 Borrowdale Drive, Norwich, NR1 4NS   01603 927315

Wroxham Angling. Station Rd, Norwich, NR12 8UR   01603 782453

Keep a record of all your fishing trips with

Log-it

Venue:		Address:			Date:
Peg No:	Start Time:	End Time:		Weather Conditions:	

Species	Weight	Method	Rig set up	Ground Bait	Hook Bait	Time

Venue:		Address:			Date:
Peg No:	Start Time:		End Time:	Weather Conditions:	

Species	Weight	Method	Rig set up	Ground Bait	Hook Bait	Time

Venue:		Address:				Date:
Peg No:	Start Time:	End Time:		Weather Conditions:		

Species	Weight	Method	Rig set up	Ground Bait	Hook Bait	Time

F I S H I N G   T E R M S

Here is a list of the words most commonly used. This will help anglers new to the sport to understand fishing terms used by other anglers.

BALE ARM: A revolving arm on a fixed spool reel which winds line onto the spool.

BAGGING UP: A term used when an angler is catching really well, or to describe a venue that is fishing well.

BAIT BANDS: These are small rubber bands. They are aimed at securing difficult to hook baits to the hook. They come in various sizes to accommodate the size of the bait.

BAITING NEEDLE: These pull the hair loop through the bait. They have a mechanism for attaching to the loop whether it is like a small hook, or a pivot that hooks over the loop. The needle is then drawn back through the bait taking the loop and hair with it.

BARBLESS: A type of hook without sharp barbs to help retain bait and fish. Barbed hooks are banned from most fisheries.

BIN LIDS: A slang term for large bream.

BITE ALARMS: These are electronic sensors that detect the movement of line caused by the fish. They usually have an audible alarm or light to alert the angler.

BIVIES: These are domed tents with an opening at the front providing a shelter from the elements.

BOILIES: These are generally hard balls of bait that are primarily designed as a carp bait.

BREAD PUNCH: A bread punch has a circular 'punch' at the end which is pushed down onto a slice of bread and cuts a small piece out which is placed on the hook. There are many different sizes of punches for different hook sizes.

BREAKING STRAIN: The amount of pressure a line will take before snapping.

BUMPED OFF: This term is used by pole anglers, whereby through the use of heavy tactics the fish once hooked is bumped off. This happens when the fish is not big enough to expand the elastic fully.

CASTERS: The chrysalis form of a maggot.

DEADBAITING: The use of dead fish for catching predatory fish such pike, perch, and eels.

DISGORGER: A long device to help remove the hook from a fish's mouth. Always have one with you.

FOUL HOOKED: A fish that has been hooked anywhere else on the body apart from the mouth.

GROUNDBAIT: A dry mixture intended to be thrown into the water to attract fish. Usually consists of bread crumb, crushed biscuit, crushed hemp or other ingredients.

HAIR RIG: A hair rig is generally a piece of line that extends beyond the point of the shank of the hook. On the end of the length of line is a small loop.

HOOKLENGTH: A short length of line, of lesser breaking strength than the mainline, to which the hook is tied. It is used to make it less likely to be detected by the fish. It also ensures that if the line is snapped by a fish, the angler would not then lose the float / swim feeder / leger and all the other shot

Legering: Bait held on the bottom by means of a weight or feeder.

Loosefeed: Small offerings of loose bait, such as maggots or sweetcorn, which are thrown into the water to keep the fish interested in the area you are fishing.

Line bites: False indications of bites usually caused by fish brushing against the line.

Lures: Artificial fish, used to tempt predators such as pike and zander.

Margin: This is an area nearest the bank, that has a shallower depth than that of the main water.

Match fishing: A competitive form of coarse fishing which involves people drawing out a random peg (a place to fish), and then trying to catch as many fish as possible within the allotted time. Usually the winner will be the one with the greatest weight of fish caught.

Peg: A peg is a pre defined fishing area. Venues are split up into evenly spaced fishing zones which are often marked with a wooden peg or marker.

Pinkies: The larvae of the green bottle fly. Small, very lively and great as a loosefeed on stillwaters and canals or as a hookbait for smaller fish.

Plummet: A device used for determining the depth of the water in which you are fishing.

Pole: A pole is constructed from very advanced carbon combinations and comes in various sizes, weight and prices.

Pole rig: These are lengths of line that have the float, weights and a hook attached.

Quiver tip: A special type of rod used to detect bites when ledgering. It has a sensitive tip that curves over when the angler has a bite. Quiver tips vary in strength and stiffness which can be changed according to the weather conditions.

Snags: Features in your swim that are likely to cause you problems They can also be fish holding features such as lilies, overhanging trees, sunken branches. A place to avoid once a fish is hooked.

Spade end hooks: Spade end hooks have an up-turned flattened piece of metal instead of an eye to which to tie the fishing line.

Specimen: A term given to any fish that is a particularly good size for its species.

Strike: To respond to the taking of the bait by pulling the rod in an upwards or sideways motion to hook the fish.

Swim: The area of water where you are fishing.

Tackle: A term used to refer to any fishing equipment (photo tackle)

Test curve: The test curve is the time and weight needed to make the tip bend 90 degrees from the rod butt. Each rod has a test curve with those being used for specimen fish such as carp having a greater test curve than a general coarse rod.

Trotting: Allowing a float to travel at the speed of the current.

Whip: This is a scaled down version of a pole.

F I S H E R Y   I N D E X

page no.

Airfield Lakes 9

Barford Lakes 10

Bartles Lodge 11

Billingford Fishing Lakes 12

Burgh Castle Fisheries 13

Buttonhole Lake 14

Catch 22 Fishing Centrel 15

Chapel Road Lake 16

Church Meadow Ponds 17

Cobbleacre Lakes 18

Cross Drove Coarse Fishery 19

Deer's Glade 20

Dents of Hilgay 21

Dilham Fishery 22

Felthorpe Lakes 23

Fendick's Fishery 24

Heartsmere Pool 25

Hevingham Lakes 26

Marshview Fishing Lake 27

Mill Road Fishery 28

Narborough Coarse Lakes 29

Oakwood Park Lakes 30

Oxborough Fishing Lakes 31

Park Farm Lakes 32

Pocahontas Lake 33

Rectory Farm Lakes 34

Reepham Fishery 35

Rocklands Mere Fishery 36

Shallowbrook Fishing Lakes 37

South Creake Fishing Lakes 38

Stanninghall lakes 39

Swangey Lakes 40

Swanton Morley Fishery 41

Taswood Lakes 42

Taverham Mill Fishery 43

The Bridge Inn Fishery 44

Turf Hole Pond 45

Willowcroft Fishery 46

Woodlakes 47

River Ant 48

River Bure 48

River Yare 49

If you know of a fishery that you would like including in one of these fish-it guides or you want to update an existing venue. Please fill in the form below.

Fishery Name

Fishery Address

Post code

Contact Name

Telephone No

Adult Day Ticket Price	£	concession OAP'S	£

Fish species and approximate weights

Brief Description

Rules / Bans

Facilities

Number of Lakes

Please e-mail or post a colour photo for inclusion in the next publication.

Please return this form to:
Arc Publishing
166 Knowle Lane,
Bents Green,
Sheffield S11 9SJ.

chris_keeling@tiscali.co.uk

New Fishery ☐

Update to Fishery ☐

New Fishery / Fishery Update Form

63

These regional fishing guides are packed with a wide range of information on lakes, ponds, canals, reservoirs and rivers. Each venue has a full colour page detailing all you need to know for a great days fishing. There are photos of each venue as well as useful tips on which peg to fish and best baits to use.

Readers Special Offer

Enquiries 07809 172872

Any book for £7.99 each.	Saving £1.00
Any 2 books £7.50 each - total £15.00	Saving £2.98
Any 3 books £6.99 each - total £20.97	Saving £6.00
Any 4 books £6.50 each - total £26.00	Saving £9.96
Any 5 books £5.99 each - total £29.95	Saving £15.00
Any 6 books £5.50 each - total £33.00	Saving £20.94
All 7 books £4.99 each - total £34.93	**Saving £28.00**

HOW TO ORDER

Please enter your selection and quantity of books you require.

☐ Fish-it Linc's   ☐ Fish-it4 W/Y   ☐ Fish-it7 Nott's
☐ Fish-it2 S/Y   ☐ Fish-it5 N/Y   ☐ All 7 books
☐ Fish-it3 E/Y   ☐ Fish-it6 Derby

Name..

Address..

....

....

Phone No...

On orders of 1-3 books please add £2.00 to cover postage and packing.
On orders of 4-7 books please add £3.50 to cover postage and packing.

I enclose a cheque for £...............

Please make cheques payable to: CHRIS KEELING

Please send your completed form together with your cheque/postal order to:
CHRIS KEELING, 166 KNOWLE LANE, SHEFFIELD, S11 9SJ.